PROGRESSIVE SOCIAL PROTECTION

A COMPREHENSIVE GUIDE

AMIT SHUKLA

Made with ♥ on the Notion Press Platform
www.notionpress.com

This book is dedicated to all those who have dedicated their lives to advancing the cause of progressive social protection. To the activists, advocates, and politicians who have fought for economic justice and fought to ensure that everyone has access to a dignified life. To the researchers and academics who have committed their time and energy to studying and understanding the complexities of social protection and its impacts. And to the countless people who have been personally affected by social protection policies—both positively and negatively—and whose stories continue to shape our understanding of the importance of social protection. We owe it to all of you to continue our progress in building a more equitable and just world.

Contents

Foreword

In the face of increasing economic inequalities, the need for progressive social protection has never been greater. In an era of rising global poverty and inequality, the demand for social protection policies that are both effective and equitable is growing.

Progressives have long argued that social protection systems should provide a basic level of income security to all citizens, regardless of their economic or social status. At the same time, they have called for policies that promote greater economic equality and reduce poverty.

The emergence of the progressive social protection agenda has been shaped by the need to respond to the contemporary challenges of poverty and inequality. This book provides an overview of the major concepts and principles underlying the progressive social protection agenda, and examines its application in the global context.

The authors explore the different dimensions of social protection, including the role of social assistance, social insurance, and public works, as well as the broader issues of economic justice and human rights. They also discuss the challenges of designing and implementing social protection policies, focusing in particular on the need to ensure equity and inclusion. Finally, the authors consider the implications of the progressive social protection agenda for the future of social policy and the global economy.

This book is an invaluable resource for those interested in learning about the progressive social protection agenda and its implications for social policy. It is essential reading for those who are interested in understanding how the progressive social protection agenda can be used to promote greater economic justice and reduce poverty.

Preface

In the face of a rapidly changing world, progressive social protection policies have become an increasingly important part of the development landscape. As people's needs change, and the challenges they face become more complex and diverse, social protection has emerged as a key tool for governments and communities to meet these challenges.

In this book, we aim to provide an overview of the current state of progressive social protection, and to explore the potential for further development. We draw on a wide range of sources, including research, policy documents and case studies, to provide a comprehensive examination of the issues at hand.

We consider the different forms of social protection, and the way they have evolved over time. We also explore the challenges and opportunities that come with different approaches to social protection, including the need to ensure that the most vulnerable are not left behind.

Finally, we discuss the role of different actors in the development of progressive social protection, and how they can be best supported. We hope that this book will serve as a useful resource for those seeking to further develop their understanding of the concept of progressive social protection, and to better equip them to design, implement and evaluate social protection policies.

Acknowledgements

I am deeply grateful to everyone who contributed to this book. First, I must thank my editor, who was invaluable in helping me shape the book's content and structure.

I am also thankful to my research assistants, who worked diligently to ensure that the data and analysis were accurate.

I am especially grateful to the many individuals and organizations who gave me the opportunity to conduct field research on progressive social protection initiatives. Without their generosity, this book would not have been possible.

Finally, I must mention the countless advocates for social justice and progressive social protection who have worked tirelessly to improve the lives of those living in poverty. Their dedication and commitment to this cause is an inspiration to me, and I thank them for their efforts.

Prologue

The idea of social protection has been around since the dawn of civilization, when ancient societies protected their members through mutual aid arrangements and social services. Over the millennia, social protection evolved in different forms, from informal arrangements to more formal systems of public welfare.

Today, social protection is still used to protect people from poverty, unemployment, disability, old age, and other forms of deprivation. In recent years, however, the concept of social protection has experienced a revival as governments and international organizations recognize the need for a more flexible and progressive approach to social policy.

This book looks at progressive social protection, which focuses on providing social assistance tailored to the specific needs of individuals and groups. It examines the principles of progressive social protection, outlines the key components of a modern social protection system, and discusses the opportunities and challenges associated with its implementation.

Through a combination of theoretical and empirical analysis, this book sheds light on the concept of progressive social protection and demonstrates its potential for delivering greater security, opportunity, and wellbeing for all.

CHAPTER ONE

Defining Progressive Social Protection

Social protection is an integral part of human development, providing individuals with a sense of security, stability, and well-being. It is an essential element of any comprehensive approach to promote social justice, reduce poverty, and improve the quality of life for all. Yet, the concept of social protection is not clearly defined and is often used interchangeably with other related terms, such as welfare, social services, and social security. In this chapter, we will define progressive social protection and discuss its importance in advancing social justice and reducing poverty.

Definition of Progressive Social Protection

Progressive social protection is a comprehensive approach to social protection that seeks to advance social justice, reduce poverty, and improve the quality of life for all. It encompasses a wide range of social policies, interventions, and programs that provide people with access to basic services and necessities, such as health care, education, housing, and food security. It is also concerned with providing individuals with the necessary resources and support to build a secure and sustainable future.

Importance of Progressive Social Protection

Progressive social protection is essential for achieving social justice and reducing poverty. It provides individuals with the resources and support they need to build a secure and sustainable future. It also helps to reduce inequality and foster a sense of belonging and inclusion. Additionally, it can promote economic growth and stability by providing individuals with access to secure employment and training opportunities.

Conclusion

In conclusion, progressive social protection is an essential part of any comprehensive approach to promote social justice, reduce poverty, and improve the quality of life for all. It provides individuals with access to basic services and necessities, as well as the resources and support to build a secure and sustainable future. It is an important tool for achieving social justice and reducing poverty, and is essential for promoting economic growth and stability.

CHAPTER TWO

Progressive Social Protection

The concept of progressive social protection has been gaining traction in recent years as a way to better protect vulnerable populations and ensure that everyone is able to access the same level of basic rights and services. Progressive social protection involves the implementation of policies and programs that are designed to provide more equitable access to social protection services and benefits for all individuals, regardless of their income, gender, ethnicity, or other characteristics. It is a system that recognizes that all individuals should have access to social protection and that the system should be tailored to meet their specific needs.

To begin, it is important to understand the core principles of progressive social protection, which include equity, inclusion, universality, and solidarity. Equity is the principle that all people should have equal access to social protection services. Inclusion is the idea that everyone should have the opportunity to participate in the system, regardless of their background or circumstances. Universality suggests that everyone should have access to the same level of social protection services, regardless of their ability to pay. And finally, solidarity indicates that everyone should work together to ensure the system is fair and that everyone is able to benefit from it.

The next step is to look at how progressive social protection can be implemented. This can be done through the introduction of a variety of programs and policies, such as universal health care, a guaranteed basic income, and universal access to education. These types of policies are designed to ensure that everyone has equitable access to the services and benefits they need. Additionally, governments should ensure that the services and benefits are provided in an equitable and inclusive manner, such as through the use of progressive taxation and targeted spending.

Finally, it is important to note that progressive social protection is not a one-size-fits-all solution. Each country and region will have different needs and should tailor the system to meet those needs. Additionally, it is important to recognize that progressive social protection is not a static system, but one that needs to be adapted over time to ensure it remains effective.

Progressive social protection is an important concept that has the potential to make a real difference in the lives of vulnerable populations. By understanding the core principles of progressive social protection and implementing targeted policies and programs, governments can ensure that everyone is able to access the same level of basic rights and services.

CHAPTER THREE

The Benefits of Progressive Social Protection

The term "progressive" describes social protection systems designed to be more equitable, inclusive, and effective than traditional systems. A progressive social protection system is one that is tailored to the needs of those most in need, and which allows for adjustments over time to meet changing circumstances. This type of system typically involves a combination of cash transfers, in-kind transfers, and public services, such as health and education.

Progressive social protection systems are important for several reasons. First, they provide a safety net for those in need, allowing them access to essential resources they would not otherwise be able to obtain. Secondly, they help reduce poverty and inequality, as they provide resources to those most in need and ensure that everyone can reach their full potential. Finally, progressive social protection systems can help to build stronger and more cohesive communities, by providing a sense of stability and security to those in need.

In order to ensure that all citizens have access to the resources they need, governments need to put in place robust and effective progressive social protection systems. This requires significant investment, both in terms of financial resources and in terms of building the necessary infrastructure and capacity. However, the long-term benefits of such an approach are clear. Investing in progressive social protection systems can ensure that everyone has the opportunity to reach their full potential, and can help to build more inclusive, equitable, and prosperous societies.

Progressive social protection is an important tool for reducing inequality and poverty. It provides a universal floor of protection that can be strengthened over time through targeted interventions. This type of social protection has several benefits, including:

1. Improved Health: With the implementation of progressive social protection, individuals have access to improved health care and nutrition, leading to better overall health outcomes. This can lead to a decrease in overall health-care costs for society, as well as reduced absenteeism from work and school.

2. Greater Opportunity: Progressive social protection can open up opportunities for individuals to gain skills and access education, enabling them to improve their economic situations and become more productive members of society.

3. More Economic Security: Progressive social protection can provide individuals with greater economic security, reducing poverty and promoting economic growth. It can also help reduce economic inequality, as less well-off people are more likely to benefit from such protection.

4. Increased Social Stability: With the implementation of progressive social protection, individuals have access to improved security, reducing the risk of poverty and social unrest. This can help to create a more stable environment, in which economic growth and social progress are more likely to occur.

Overall, progressive social protection is an important tool for reducing inequality and poverty, while promoting economic growth and social progress. It can provide individuals with improved security and greater opportunities, while helping to create a more stable environment.

CHAPTER FOUR

Implementing Progressive Social Protection

The implementation of progressive social protection is a complex process that requires a multi-sectoral approach. It involves a wide range of actors, including government, civil society and the private sector, as well as international organizations and donors. It also requires a long-term commitment to developing, strengthening and sustaining social protection systems.

This chapter will discuss the key elements of implementing progressive social protection. It will consider the role of each actor in the process and the various approaches that can be taken. It will look at the challenges and opportunities associated with progressive social protection and the importance of monitoring and evaluation.

1. Developing and Strengthening Social Protection Systems The development and strengthening of progressive social protection systems requires a long-term commitment to the process. This includes creating an enabling

environment for social protection, developing and strengthening social protection policies, and building the capacity of governments, civil society and the private sector to deliver social protection services.

A. Creating an Enabling Environment Creating an enabling environment for progressive social protection requires a commitment from all stakeholders to ensure that social protection is a priority in the national development agenda. This includes engaging key stakeholders in the policy-making process, raising public awareness on the importance of social protection, and ensuring that social protection policies are accessible and equitable.

B. Developing and Strengthening Social Protection Policies Developing and strengthening social protection policies involves designing policies that are targeted, equitable and cost-effective, and that are adapted to the country context. It also involves ensuring that policies are implemented effectively and developing mechanisms to monitor and evaluate the impact of social protection policies.

C. Building Capacity Building capacity involves developing the skills and knowledge of government, civil society and the private sector to deliver social protection services. This includes training and capacity building for civil servants, strengthening the capacity of civil society organizations, and creating an enabling environment for the private sector to play an active role in the delivery of social protection services.

2. Approaches to Implementation The implementation of progressive social protection requires an integrated approach involving different approaches and tools. These approaches include:

A. Targeted Approaches Targeted approaches involve targeting social protection services to specific groups, such as the poor and vulnerable, through means-testing and other forms of targeting. This can help to ensure that social protection services are accessible to those who need them most, while also helping to reduce poverty and inequality.

B. Universal Approaches Universal approaches involve providing social protection services to everyone, regardless of their income or other characteristics. This can help to ensure that everyone has access to social protection services, while also reducing inequality and poverty.

C. Social Insurance Approaches Social insurance approaches involve providing social protection services through insurance-based mechanisms. This can help to ensure that social protection services are accessible and equitable, while also helping to reduce poverty and inequality.

3. Challenges and Opportunities Implementing progressive social protection is associated with challenges and opportunities. These include:

A. Financial Challenges The development and implementation of progressive social protection policies can be costly, especially in terms of the resources required to build capacity and strengthen institutional frameworks. This can be a particular challenge in countries with limited resources.

B. Political Challenges Political challenges can arise due to a lack of political will or commitment to social protection. This can be a particular challenge in countries with weak governments and a lack of accountability.

C. Social Challenges Social challenges can arise due to a lack of public awareness or acceptance of social protection policies. This can be a particular challenge in countries with a history of exclusion or marginalization.

D. Opportunities Implementing progressive social protection can create significant opportunities for poverty reduction, economic growth and social development. It can also help to create more equitable and inclusive societies while also helping to reduce inequality.

4. Monitoring and Evaluation Monitoring and evaluation are essential for successfully implementing progressive social protection. This involves collecting and analyzing data on the impact of social protection policies and assessing the effectiveness, efficiency and equity of social protection services. This can help to ensure that social protection policies are effective, cost-effective and equitable.

Conclusion

Implementing progressive social protection is a complex process requiring a multi-sectoral approach. It involves a wide range of actors, including government, civil society and the private sector, as well as international organizations and donors. It also requires a long-term commitment to developing, strengthening and sustaining social protection systems. The implementation process involves creating an enabling environment, developing and strengthening social protection policies, and building the capacity of governments, civil society and the private sector to deliver social protection services. It also requires an integrated approach that combines different approaches and tools. Implementing progressive social protection is associated with challenges and opportunities, and it is essential to monitor and evaluate the impact of social protection policies.

CHAPTER FIVE

Challenges of Progressive Social Protection

The idea of progressive social protection has been gaining traction in recent years, and its implementation has been growing in countries around the world. However, there are still many challenges that must be faced in order to ensure that the concept of progressive social protection is fully embraced and realized.

One of the biggest challenges is the need for adequate funding. All social protection programs require significant financial resources in order to be successful, and many of the more progressive programs may require even more funding than traditional programs. Governments may be unwilling to provide these necessary funds, or they may not have the capacity to do so. This means that alternative sources of financing, such as international donors and philanthropic organizations, must be used in order to ensure that the necessary funds are available.

Another challenge is the need to address the issue of inequality. Many of the more progressive social protection programs are designed to reduce inequality and provide better access to services for vulnerable populations. However, these programs can often be undermined by existing inequalities within society. This means that in order to make sure that these programs are successful, governments must address the underlying structural and institutional issues that contribute to inequality and marginalization.

Finally, there is the challenge of ensuring that the programs are effectively implemented. The success of any social protection program depends on the ability of governments to effectively implement it. This can be difficult, as there are often competing interests and political considerations that must be taken into account when designing and implementing a program. In addition, the lack of capacity or resources can also be a major obstacle.

Ultimately, the challenges of progressive social protection are significant, but they are not insurmountable. With the right combination of political will and financial resources, these challenges can be overcome and progressive social protection can be successfully implemented.

CHAPTER SIX

Maximizing Benefits of Progressive Social Protection

The concept of progressive social protection is gaining more and more momentum in recent years. It is being increasingly seen as an important tool to reduce global poverty and enhance the economic security of individuals and families. While the traditional social protection systems focus on providing basic entitlements, progressive social protection takes a more holistic approach to poverty reduction. It recognizes the importance of enabling people to access social protection schemes that not only provide basic entitlements, but also support people to build their own economic security.

The goal of progressive social protection is to reduce poverty and inequality in a responsible and sustainable way. This requires a comprehensive approach that takes into account the different needs and contexts of people living in different countries. In order to maximize the benefits of progressive social protection, it is important to ensure that it is implemented in a well-coordinated manner.

This involves setting up effective and integrated social protection systems that are tailored to the local context and needs.

The implementation of progressive social protection should involve a range of different stakeholders, including governments, international organizations, civil society, the private sector, and local communities. All these stakeholders should work in a coordinated manner to ensure that the social protection system is effective and equitable. This will involve the development of a comprehensive and sustainable social protection system that covers a range of different areas, such as health, education, employment, and social security.

The implementation of progressive social protection should also involve the use of innovative and evidence-based approaches to poverty reduction. This involves the use of data and research to inform the design and implementation of social protection systems. It also requires an understanding of the unique needs of different groups of people and the development of tailored social protection policies that meet those needs.

Finally, it is important to ensure that there are clear goals and objectives for the implementation of progressive social protection. This will involve setting specific targets and benchmarks that can be used to track the progress of the system over time. This will help to ensure that the system is working as intended and that it is achieving its objectives.

In conclusion, progressive social protection is a powerful tool for reducing global poverty and enhancing economic security. It is important to ensure that it is implemented in a well-coordinated manner in order to maximize its benefits. This involves the active involvement of a range of stakeholders and the use of innovative and evidence-based approaches to poverty reduction. It also involves the setting of clear goals and objectives and the use of data and research to inform the design and implementation of the system.

Conclusion

The concept of progressive social protection is one that has been gaining traction in recent years. It is a concept that seeks to ensure that everyone has access to the basic necessities of life and to provide a safety net for those in need. This concept has been implemented in various countries around the world and has had a positive impact on the lives of many people.

Progressive social protection is a complex concept and has many facets, including the provision of cash transfers, health care, and education. It is important that the implementation of progressive social protection be tailored to the specific needs of the country, while also taking into account the economic, social, and political realities of the environment.

Overall, progressive social protection is a concept that has the potential to help reduce poverty and inequality, while also promoting economic growth and social stability. It is a concept that should be further explored and implemented in more countries around the world.